EXPLORING COUNTRIES

Mongolia

by Heather Adamson

BELLWETHER MEDIA · MINNEAPOLIS, MN

Note to Librarians, Teachers, and Parents:

Blastoff! Readers are carefully developed by literacy experts and combine standards-based content with developmentally appropriate text.

Level 1 provides the most support through repetition of high-frequency words, light text, predictable sentence patterns, and strong visual support.

Level 2 offers early readers a bit more challenge through varied simple sentences, increased text load, and less repetition of high-frequency words.

Level 3 advances early-fluent readers toward fluency through increased text and concept load, less reliance on visuals, longer sentences, and more literary language.

Level 4 builds reading stamina by providing more text per page, increased use of punctuation, greater variation in sentence patterns, and increasingly challenging vocabulary.

Level 5 encourages children to move from "learning to read" to "reading to learn" by providing even more text, varied writing styles, and less familiar topics.

Whichever book is right for your reader, Blastoff! Readers are the perfect books to build confidence and encourage a love of reading that will last a lifetime!

This edition first published in 2016 by Bellwether Media, Inc.

No part of this publication may be reproduced in whole or in part without written permission of the publisher. For information regarding permission, write to Bellwether Media, Inc., Attention: Permissions Department, 5357 Penn Avenue South, Minneapolis, MN 55419.

Library of Congress Cataloging-in-Publication Data

Names: Adamson, Heather, 1974- author.
Title: Mongolia / by Heather Adamson.
Description: Minneapolis, MN : Bellwether Media, Inc., 2016. | Series: Blastoff! Readers: Exploring Countries | Includes bibliographical references and index. | Audience: Ages 7-12.
Identifiers: LCCN 2015028731 | ISBN 9781626173446 (hardcover : alk. paper)
Subjects: LCSH: Mongolia–Juvenile literature.
Classification: LCC DS798 .A57 2016 | DDC 951.7/3–dc23
LC record available at http://lccn.loc.gov/2015028731

Printed in the United States of America, North Mankato, MN.

Contents

Mongolia is a **landlocked** country in Asia. Russia borders it to the north. China sits to its south. Mongolia is not even half the size of Russia or China. However, it is still large. It covers an area of 603,909 square miles (1,564,116 square kilometers).

Russia

Ulaanbaatar
★

Mongolia

China

The largest city is the capital, Ulaanbaatar. It lies in north-central Mongolia. Between the late seventeenth and early twentieth centuries, China ruled Mongolia. Back then, it was called Outer Mongolia. A part of China is still known as Inner Mongolia today.

steppe

Three mountain ranges rise in the Mongolian landscape. The largest is the Altai Mountains in the western end. Forests and lakes are scattered in the northern mountains. The Gobi Desert covers the southern third of Mongolia. One of Mongolia's most unique land features is a vast **plain**. Nearly half of Mongolia is covered in this dry region called the **steppe**.

Weather in Mongolia is extreme. Northern winters can reach -40 degrees Fahrenheit (-40 degrees Celsius). Summers in the south are often over 100 degrees Fahrenheit (38 degrees Celsius). Winds sweep across much of the land. Most days are sunny, but a dust storm, snowstorm, or rainstorm can move in fast.

Altai Mountains

The Gobi Desert spans 500,000 square miles (1,300,000 square kilometers). It covers parts of China and Mongolia. The Gobi is dry and dusty but does not have many large **dunes** of sand. Few plants live there. Saxaul trees survive by storing water under their bark.

Summers in the Gobi are hot. But the desert can also be cold. Winter temperatures are often below 0 degrees Fahrenheit (-18 degrees Celsius). The Gobi Desert is home to animals that have adapted to the cold, dry climate. Jerboas, wolves, and marbled polecats make up some of this desert's wildlife. Long ago, dinosaurs also used to live where the Gobi is today. The desert has preserved **fossils** of their eggs and bones.

fossil

golden eagle

snow leopard

Bactrian camel

Despite the dry landscape, a lot of wildlife roams Mongolia. Gazelles, saiga antelopes, and other deer are common. Snow leopards live in the mountains and desert, and wolves are found everywhere. All kinds of birds make homes in Mongolia. Birds of prey such as eagles and hawks often eat desert rodents. The steppe supports cranes, partridges, and larks.

takhi

Mongolia is also home to a few rare animals. The world's only true wild horse, the Przewalski's horse, or *takhi*, comes from Mongolia. The Gobi bear and the two-humped Bactrian camel are **native** to the Gobi Desert. The country is working hard to keep these animals alive and well.

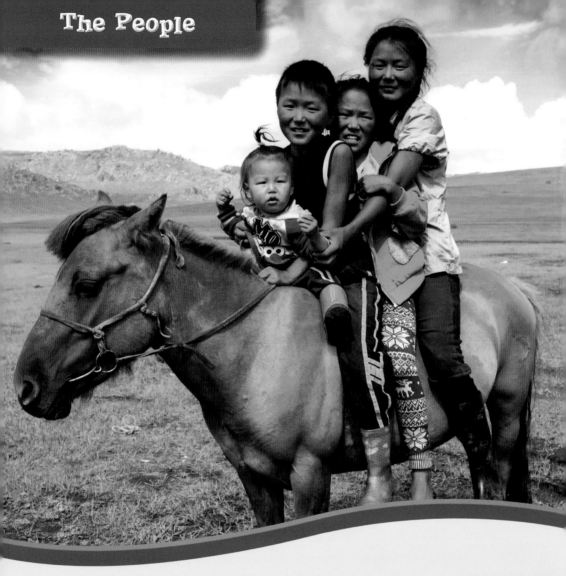

Mongols are native people of the land. Most citizens of Mongolia today come from the **traditional** culture and speak Mongolian **dialects**. Small groups from nearby areas also make the country their home. Turkic, Russian, and Chinese backgrounds are the most common. **Urban** areas often use English and Russian languages as well as Mongolian.

More than half of all Mongolians are Buddhists. Islam, Christianity, and a traditional faith of **Shamanism** are also followed. For much of the 1900s, Mongolians could not practice religion freely. Many Mongolians today still do not claim any religion. However, all Mongolians are known for their **hospitality**. They help one another survive in a tough climate. Sharing meals and stories with strangers is not uncommon.

Speak Mongolian!

The Mongolian language uses a different alphabet than English. However, Mongolian words can be written in the English alphabet so you can read them out loud.

English	Mongolian	How to say it
hello	sain baina uu	SAN BAN OH
good-bye	bayartai	BAI-YER-TAI
yes	tiim	team
no	ugui	oo-GWEE
please	üü	OH
thank you	bayarlalaa	BAI-YER-LAH
friend	naiz	NEZ

ger

Did you know?

Gers have circular wood frames that are covered with thick felt. Their construction offers good protection from wind and extreme temperatures.

About a third of Mongolia's population lives a simple **nomadic** lifestyle. They move their homes with the cattle they herd. Circular tents called *gers* are traditional homes. Nomads can pack up their gers and move in just a few hours. Still, most of Mongolia's population lives in or near cities. There, most people live in small apartments. Some prefer life in a ger. Clusters of gers can be found outside the city or next to houses in town.

There are not many paved roads across Mongolia. One railroad runs through the country from north to south. Most people travel on horses, camels, or small motorbikes. If people travel in cars, they always take a spare tire and extra parts along.

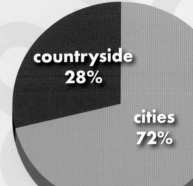

Where People Live in Mongolia

countryside 28%

cities 72%

ДЕБИЕТ — ӨМІР айнасы.

Did you know?

Mongolia is creative in bringing education to families that must move around. Movable ger classrooms, lessons for cell phones and computers, and boarding schools are ways the country offers education to everyone.

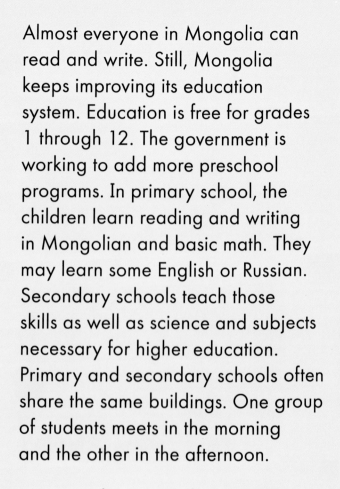

Almost everyone in Mongolia can read and write. Still, Mongolia keeps improving its education system. Education is free for grades 1 through 12. The government is working to add more preschool programs. In primary school, the children learn reading and writing in Mongolian and basic math. They may learn some English or Russian. Secondary schools teach those skills as well as science and subjects necessary for higher education. Primary and secondary schools often share the same buildings. One group of students meets in the morning and the other in the afternoon.

Many students attend universities. The National University of Mongolia in Ulaanbaatar trains students to be teachers, doctors, and engineers. Technical schools teach students specific skills for areas such as mining and energy management.

Where People Work in Mongolia

manufacturing 21%

farming 28.6%

services 50.4%

Work in Mongolia is changing. Some livestock herders still live simple lives of travel. But many also raise goods to sell in the cities. More people are beginning to work in **manufacturing**. They make wool, cashmere, and leather goods. Gold, coal, and copper mines are other growing work places. Workers dig these **natural resources** from the ground.

Under Russian control, many teachers, doctors, and veterinarians came from Russia. Now Mongolians serve in these jobs. **Tourism** is another new opportunity for **service jobs**. Hotel workers, travel guides, and cooks provide for Mongolia's guests.

Mongolians enjoy telling stories and visiting over meals. Traditional sports such as archery, horse racing, and wrestling are favorite pastimes. Mongolians have also invented many games using ankle bones of sheep and goats. They roll them like dice, flick them, and toss them. Basketball and video games are popular in the cities.

Mongolians also have unique traditional music. A square, two-stringed fiddle is a **symbol** of Mongolia. A horse head is carved out of the handle. Throat singers often play the instruments while they perform. These musicians can sing low and high tones at the same time. The sounds mimic nature.

! fun fact

A Mongolian "long song" stretches out the sound of each syllable. It may take a few minutes just to sing a word or two.

Did you know?

Mongolians are eating fruits and vegetables more often. They know the importance of a healthy diet. They have even started gardens for growing foods like cabbage.

Meat and dairy are the main foods for Mongolians. This comes from their wandering traditions. The people followed the animals and could not stay put to tend gardens. Today, beef, **mutton**, goat, and wild **game** such as gazelle are common meats. Cheese, yogurt, and curds are favorite dairy products. *Suutei tsai*, a salty milk tea, is a traditional drink.

Mongolians do often eat potatoes, carrots, and onions in a dish called *horhog*. Hunks of meat and vegetables are cooked with hot stones in a tin can. This stew is a favorite for sharing with friends at picnics. *Buuz* are popular snacks. These dough pouches are stuffed with meat and steamed.

horhog

buuz

Did you know?

Legend says that a woman once dressed as a man and won the Naadam wrestling competition. Now, wrestlers wear an open-chest wrestling shirt called a *zodog* to prevent women from wrestling in the manly games.

Naadam festival

Mongolia has few national holidays. Under Russian control, its people did not celebrate their special days. Even so, Mongolians have a few proud traditions. *Tsagaan Sar* observes the end of winter. It is a Lunar New Year holiday in January or February. This celebration of family history lasts for 15 days. People wear new traditional-style clothes. They share a lot of food and stories.

fun fact

Genghis Khan was a bold warrior who took over and united many tribes. He created a large empire in the early 13th century. His name is thought to mean "universal leader."

Mongolia's **Revolution** Day is celebrated on July 11 with the *Naadam* festival. This day revolves around horse racing, wrestling, and archery, known as Mongolia's three manly games. The country also recently created a National Pride Day on November 23 to honor historic ruler Chinggis Khaan, or Genghis Khan.

Hunting with eagles has been passed down for generations of Mongolian Kazakhs. When a boy is 13, he takes a young golden eagle from its nest. He feeds it and trains it to be his hunting partner.

On the hunt, the eagle's eyes are covered until the hunter spots prey such as a fox. He then whistles and uncovers the eagle. The eagle catches the prey, and the pair shares the meat. The eagle lives with the hunter and his family for about eight years. Then the eagle is released to live out the rest of its life in the wild. Eagle hunting is just one of many ways Mongolians show pride in their culture.

! fun fact

Tradition has been that only boys are trained to hunt with eagles. However, the daughter of one honored hunter is learning the skill. She may become Mongolia's first eagle huntress.

Fast Facts About Mongolia

Mongolia's Flag

Mongolia's flag has three equal rectangles. The two outside rectangles are red and the middle one is blue. Red stands for progress and freedom, and blue represents the sky. The national emblem is in the middle of the red rectangle on the flagpole side. The shapes on the emblem represent fire, the sun, the moon, earth, and water. The yin-yang symbol stands for harmony.

Official Name: Mongolia

Area: 603,909 square miles (1,564,116 square kilometers); Mongolia is the 19th largest country in the world.

Capital City:	Ulaanbaatar
Important Cities:	Erdenet, Darkhan
Population:	2,992,908 (July 2015)
Official Language:	Khalkha Mongol
National Holiday:	Revolution Day; Naadam festival (July 11)
Religions:	Buddhist (53%), Muslim (3%), Christian (2.2%), Shamanist (2.9%), other (0.3%), none (38.6%)
Major Industries:	herding, farming, mining, services
Natural Resources:	copper, gold, coal, oil, livestock
Manufactured Products:	construction materials, cashmere, textiles, food products
Farm Products:	wheat, barley, vegetables, sheep, goats, cattle
Unit of Money:	tögrög (also spelled tugrik)

Glossary

dialects—unique ways of speaking a language; dialects are often specific to certain regions of a country.

dunes—hills of sand

fossils—the remains of ancient plants and animals that have been preserved in stone

game—wild animals hunted for food or sport

hospitality—a generous and friendly way of treating guests

landlocked—completely surrounded by land

manufacturing—a field of work in which people use machines to make products

mutton—sheep meat

native—originally from a specific place

natural resources—materials in the earth that are taken out and used to make products or fuel

nomadic—having no specific home and traveling from place to place

plain—a large area of flat land

revolution—an uprising of people who change the form of their country's government

service jobs—jobs that perform tasks for people or businesses

Shamanism—a religion following certain people who are believed to have a connection to the spirit world and powers of healing

steppe—a wide, flat, treeless plain

symbol—something that stands for something else; the two-stringed fiddle is one symbol of Mongolia.

tourism—the business of people traveling to visit other places

traditional—related to a custom, idea, or belief handed down from one generation to the next

urban—related to cities and city life

To Learn More

AT THE LIBRARY
Aloian, Molly. *The Gobi Desert*. New York, N.Y.: Crabtree Publishing Company, 2013.

Cheng, Pang Guek. *Mongolia*. New York, N.Y.: Marshall Cavendish Benchmark, 2010.

Hotchkiss, Gerald G. *Emily in Khara Koto: A Young Girl's Adventure in Mongolia*. Santa Fe, N.M.: Sunstone Press, 2014.

ON THE WEB
Learning more about Mongolia is as easy as 1, 2, 3.

1. Go to www.factsurfer.com.

2. Enter "Mongolia" into the search box.

3. Click the "Surf" button and you will see a list of related web sites.

With factsurfer.com, finding more information is just a click away.

Index

The images in this book are reproduced through the courtesy of: alenvl, front cover; Maisei Raman, front cover (flag), p. 28; loca4motion, p. 6; aleksandr hunta, pp. 7, 10 (bottom); Stock Connection/ SuperStock, p. 8; Tuul & Bruno Morandi/ Corbis, p. 9; jurra8, p. 10 (top); Dennis W. Donohue, p. 10 (middle); loflo69, p. 11; Eleanor Scriven/ Glow Images, p. 12; Pierre-Jean Durieu, p. 14; Maxim Petrichuk, p. 15; Martti Putkonen/ SuperStock, p. 16; Dmitry Chulov, p. 18; Philippe Michel/ age fotostock/ SuperStock, p. 19 (left); Egmont Strigl/ Glow Images, p. 19 (right); Hugh Sitton/ Corbis, p. 20; Nick Rains/ Corbis, p. 21; Sophie Dauwe, p. 22; Fanfo, p. 23 (left); Mizu_Basyo/ Wikipedia, p. 23 (right); robertharding/ Alamy, pp. 24-25; Rentsendorj Bazarsukh/ Corbis, p. 25; Josef Friedhuber, p. 27; Don Norris/ Wikipedia, p. 29 (top); Oleg_Mit, p. 29 (bottom).